The Warrior Marketer

Copyright © 2016

All rights reserved. No part of this book may be reproduced, stored in a retrieval system, or transmitted in any form or by any means, electronic, mechanical, photocopying, recording, scanning, or otherwise, without the prior written permission of the publisher.

Disclaimer

All the material contained in this book is provided for educational and informational purposes only. No responsibility can be taken for any results or outcomes resulting from the use of this material.

While every attempt has been made to provide information that is both accurate and effective, the author does not assume any responsibility for the accuracy or use/misuse of this information.

You are encouraged to print this book for easy reading.

Use this information at your own risk.

Contents

Introduction 7

What Is Your Why? 13

Fighting The Curse of Unrealistic Expectations 17

A Warrior Keeps His Promises 20

Sharpen Your Sword 22
- 3 tasks a day 23
- Doing just enough to be a little uncomfortable 24
- Do the most difficult task first 25
- Activity and work are two different things 26
- Know when to take a break 26
- The Importance of Focus 27

Battling The Fear Demons 29
1. Fear of the Unknown 31
2. The Fear of Failure 34
3. The Fear That You Are Not Good Enough 37
4. The Fear That You're Late or Too Old 40
5. Limiting Beliefs 41

Climb The Staircase That You Can't See 45
- Visualize your success 46
- Prayer is powerful 47

- Read autobiographies of successful people 48
- Motivate yourself regularly 48

A Tiger Doesn't Lose Sleep Over The Opinions Of Sheep. 50

- Look at your why 51
- Remember the bamboo tree 52
- Get motivated 53
- Know that it's all turbulence 53
- Success turns naysayers into supporters 54
- Understand the psychology behind it 54

Weight Loss Is Simpler Than You Think 56

1. Cut the carbs 60
2. Intermittent fasting 62
3. Get enough sleep 65
4. Fasted cardio 66
5. Shorter but higher intensity workouts 68
6. Eat Foods That Burn Fat 70
7. Drink Lots of Water 72
8. Have a Food Journal 73

From Ideal Weight To A Six Pack 75

Calories 76
Training 77
Diet 79

Building Muscle and Gaining Mass 83

How many reps and sets? 85
How much muscle can I hope to gain? 88
Before you start with weights 89
Don't neglect your posture and flexibility 90

A Warrior Watches His Money 92
- What's your number? 93
- Money is oxygen to your business 94
- Can you do both effectively? 95
- Your six month nest egg 95
- Insurance and medical benefits 96
- Is your spouse working? 96

The Biggest Secret To Making Money Online 98
What's shiny object syndrome? 99
- Most of it is noise 100
- Focus on just one method 101
- Stick to proven products and reputable sellers 102
- Get the right tools only 102
- Segment your emails 103

When The Warrior Fails 105
1. Don't take it personally 108
2. Learn From Your Mistakes 110
3. Stop Dwelling On Your Failures 111
4. Model Other Marketers 112
5. Assess Your Finances 114
6. Release the Need for Approval from Others 116
7. Take a Break 117

What It All Comes Down To 120
- Be organized 121
- Master the fundamentals 121
- Stick to the basics 122
- Always have a backup plan 123
- Stay grounded 123

Be A Warrior, Not a Worrier 126

Introduction

"A fine line separates a **FIGHTER** from a **WARRIOR**. One is motivated by reason, the other by purpose. One fights to live, while the other lives to fight."

Hopefully, the quote above inspired you and made you realize that this book that you're reading now is unlike any other. It was written with internet marketers in mind because most of them face certain issues that are very unique.

While most self-help books will congratulate you on taking action and buying these books… that's not going to happen here. All too often, a quote by Lao Tzu is tossed around just to make people feel good… *"A journey of a thousand miles begins with a single step."*

People read this quote and feel very happy when they take the first step. Every New Year's Day, millions of people decide to lose weight and get fit. Their 'single step' involves them paying money and signing up for a gym membership.

This explains why most gyms make most of their money in December and January. The gyms are packed in January with people taking their single step. By March, these same gyms have become ghost towns.

Why? Why does this happen?

The answer is simple. People focus on the wrong part of the quote. They focus on the words 'single step' instead of the most important word... "*A journey of a thousand miles begins with a single step.*"

'Begins' is the most important word in that quote. Anybody can take that single step and most people do. What happens after that? What happens when you realize that the thousand mile journey probably requires you to take 10,000 steps?

Will you carry on? Will you take all the steps that you need to?

The hard truth is that most people don't. The journey seems too long. The promise doesn't seem clear any more. Results aren't coming fast enough... and discouragement sets in.

They quit once the initial sparkle of the first step gets dull. They lose interest and throw in the towel and decide that it's just not worth the effort.

... Until New Year's Day comes around again the following year.

This book will put the fire in your heart to keep going when skies seem dark and the struggles are real. It will give you the strength and guidance to go from the first step to the last one where you attain your goals and dreams.

Thousands of people get on the internet to try and make money. Most quit within the first few months. Out of those who do stay, the majority quit within the first year.

Those who do become successful often realize their goal by sacrificing their health and time with their family. Their business consumes all of their time.

The majority of online marketers are overweight or struggle with health issues. This is not a coincidence. The very nature of online marketing requires one to go through a steep learning curve and it's also very time consuming.

The initial stages of building a business is hard work before you reach a stage where you can automate your business and earn a passive income. There's just no escaping this fact.

Marketers do their best to do as much as they can at the expense of everything else. There seems to be no other way because of the nature of the internet marketing beast.

This book will show you that being fit and being successful online are not mutually exclusive. You can build a six figure business and six pack abs at the same time.

You just need to know the right techniques and the shortcuts so that you do what matters when it matters. This book will teach you simple but highly effective techniques to shed the excess pounds.

Want to build muscle? No problem. You'll discover time saving methods that will get you there as soon as possible.

Trying to get a washboard stomach that will turn heads? That's covered too.

This book will also cover the emotional and mental issues that so many marketers go through in their online journey. You'll learn to develop mental toughness and resilience to weather the constant challenges that come your way.

There is no fluff and untested theory here. If something can be said it two words, I didn't use three. The methods here work, if you work them.

Make a promise to yourself that you'll complete this book and apply what you learn. Knowledge is like paint. It does no good until it's applied.

"Victorious warriors win first and then go to war, while defeated warriors go to war first and then seek to win." – Sun Tzu

What Is Your Why?

Knowing your why will make all the difference. So what is this 'why' that we're talking about?

It's your reason for doing what you do and make no mistake about this - Your why will always have an emotional reason. You need to dig deep to discover why you want what you want.

If you want to get lean and fit, ask yourself why you want to do it. Be honest. Most people do not want to get in shape for health reasons... That's so boring. Oh no no no! There's always something else.

If men want to get muscular, they probably want to turn women's heads. They want to feel desirable. The same applies for women who want to shed the excess pounds. Maybe they want their spouse or partner to look at them in a whole new way.

There's nothing wrong with a little vanity. What matters is that you know why you want what you want.

Some people do it for bragging rights. Others want to prove their naysayers wrong. Then there are people who just want to achieve something worthy in their life so that they can have the confidence to say that they did at least one thing right.

Even a person who has had a heart attack and recovers will change his eating habits and be more active for an emotional reason. They may fear dying or they want to live so that they can see their kids grow up. **This is the REAL REASON.**

They're not doing it for the sake of being healthy. You must dig deep and self-reflect until you find your underlying reason.

Why do you want to make money online? It's probably not the numbers that excite you.

Saying that you don't have your own boss is cool. Being able to brag that nobody controls you anymore and that you live according to your own rules is really fun. Being able to buy expensive things without worrying about your finances is beyond fantastic.

These are the emotions that drive you. Your job is to find out what it is… and once you do, **WRITE IT DOWN!**

This is your Warrior Purpose.

If you want, you can even make a video where you record yourself on your mobile phone explaining why your goal is so important to you. It has to be heartfelt. You must be brutally honest with yourself.

Save the video… and keep the paper that you've written your why on. Always keep them handy.

There will come a point when you're tempted to give up on your goals and dreams. This is inevitable. The universe is challenging you. It may seem all hokey… but you can definitely expect struggles and obstacles to pop-up.

At times like these, you MUST look at the why that you've written down or recorded. Rewrite it if you have to just so you remember and feel what it is you truly wanted.

This will prevent you from throwing in the towel. It will force you to choose between what you want now and what you want most. If you're tired of starting over, then stop giving up. A warrior fights to his last. That's his purpose… Your why is your purpose.

Remember it at all times… and keep refreshing your memory when the initial excitement of taking the first step starts to wane.

Fighting The Curse of Unrealistic Expectations

This curse has probably killed more dreams than any other reason… but people bring it upon themselves.

Rome wasn't built in a day. This is a very bitter pill to swallow. Success takes time. It takes time to build a business. Losing weight takes time. Building a muscular body takes time.

However, most people are impatient. We live in a world of instant text messaging and microwaves. Everybody wants results fast and they want them now. It just doesn't work that way.

Do not lose faith just because it's taking longer than you thought it would. All things come to he who waits. Keep pushing forward in faith.

Generally, a person can lose about 1 to 2 pounds of fat a week. If you're just starting off, you may lose more initially but with time, your results will taper off and you'll probably be at the 1 to 2 pounds per week range.

What if you're 40 pounds overweight? You're looking at a 30 to 40 week stretch to reach your ideal weight. That's about 8 to 9 months!

Most people expect to lose all their excess weight in about 3 weeks. When the results don't come, they lose hope and give up. They never give it enough time.

A warrior takes years to develop his skills. Time is your greatest ally. It doesn't matter what goal you're aiming for. With persistent effort and time, you'll get to your destination.

Keep your expectations realistic. It's good to have a goal that seems out of reach so that you can strive to do your best. Just do not expect to get there overnight.

He who masters patience masters everything else. Avoid this curse at all cost and do not quit just before results start to come.

A Warrior Keeps His Promises

When we speak of keeping your promises, it's not just about keeping your promises to other people. You absolutely MUST keep your promises to yourself too.

So few people do this without realizing just how devastating the effects are. If you decide to work out thrice a week, you MUST keep this promise to yourself. If you plan to create content daily for your online business, you must stick to the plan.

There will be times when you just do not feel like it. Times when you're not in the mood. It's during these times that you must take action.

This topic will be addressed in a later chapter. For now, what you need to know is this... When you do not keep your promises to yourself, you lose respect for yourself.

You may give all the excuses you want. As convincing as they may be, deep down on a subconscious level, you'll know that you failed yourself.

Many people hate themselves for not getting to where they want to go in life. It all starts from these little promises that you don't keep.

In the next chapter we'll look at why you should do what matters, when it matters. Respect yourself, your goals and your efforts.

Once you do what you need to do, you'll feel motivated and proud of yourself. This will give you the impetus to keep pushing forward towards your goals.

Sharpen Your Sword

A warrior's sword is always sharp... and they do not sharpen it during a fight. All preparation and training is done beforehand. They're prepared and ready. They've done what mattered... and this is something that's crucial to success.

Doing what matters is so important that it literally determines if you'll succeed or just spin your wheels and go nowhere. The world is full of people who are always busy and doing things that's supposed to take them places... but they have no results to show for it.

It always seems like they're not going anywhere but they can't wait to get there. The reason for this is that they mistake activity for work. For example, if you want to lose weight, what really matters is that you workout and watch your calories.

Reading a ton of nutrition books, spending hours on YouTube picking up diet tips and joining a gym will not make you lose weight. What really matters is the training and what you're eating.

That's really all it is... and so many people don't get it. They overwhelm themselves with too much information without taking the right action. The 5 tips below will tell you exactly what you need to do to actually succeed.

- **3 tasks a day**

Don't make a list of 275 things to get done. That's enough to overwhelm anyone. Start with just 3 tasks... and it must be 3 important tasks. If you're trying to lose weight, the 3 tasks might be a 20 minute stamina workout, intermittent fasting for that day and sleeping early so that you get sufficient rest.

All you need to do are do these 3 tasks. That's it. If you did them over and over, you'll reach your weight loss goal.

Don't give yourself too much work such as studying blood type diets, seeing if the Jupiter is in alignment with Mars so that your chakras will be activated during your yoga session, etc.

All levity aside... focus on just 3 important tasks a day.

- **Doing just enough to be a little uncomfortable**

You must be challenged in order to grow. If you're trying to build a business online, that may mean writing 2,000 words of content a day. Once you get used to creating this much content with ease, you may wish to push yourself a little and aim for 2,500 words.

You want to be making gradual progress. Over time, you'll be amazed at how it all adds up.

The same applies to your fitness. If you can only run for 10 minutes on the treadmill, that's ok. With each workout, try and increase the duration by 20 seconds.

The difference will be a little uncomfortable but it won't be so bad that it scares you. Make measurable progress in reasonable time.

- **Do the most difficult task first**

It's human nature to do everything else but the most difficult task. You might decide to rearrange your desk or sort out your folders in your computer when what you really need to do is analyze the statistics in your advertising account.

The mind tries to escape the difficult tasks. Your job is to do them first. Forget everything else and just do the most difficult task at once. Focus on that. Once that is complete, it'll be a weight off your chest and the rest of the lesser tasks will be completed with ease.

- **Activity and work are two different things**

As mentioned earlier, you must know the difference. Streamline your life so that you're only doing what matters. Do not do unnecessary stuff. Eliminate all the trivial jobs that don't contribute to your progress.

Then you'll have more time to do what matters.

- **Know when to take a break**

Music is the space between the notes. Take short breaks every time you feel a little tired. This will keep you focused and more energetic to complete the important stuff.

That's really all there is to it.

"Don't tell me how busy you are. Show me what you've gotten done. Words don't matter. Results do." – Larry Winget

The Importance of Focus

Bruce Lee once said, *"Concentration is the root of all the higher abilities in man."*

To succeed in life, you must have the ability to focus and concentrate. Focused hard work is the key to success. The best way to focus is to remove all distractions.

But focus is slightly more than just removing distractions. In our day and age, multitasking is said to be a useful skill.

In truth, you should avoid multitasking. It distracts you and over time you'll lose the ability to stay focused on any one thing for long.

You'll never see a warrior engaged in a sword fight and taking quick peeps at his Facebook wall to see what's up. 100% focus on the fight in front of you.

Aim to do just one task at a time and give it your best. You must know how long you can last while concentrating. Some people can focus for an entire hour without getting exhausted… while others may get tired after just 20 minutes.

Do what suits you best. If you need a mental break, take it. Spend 5 minutes resting and come back and focus on your task again. Over time, your 'stamina' will increase.

It's crucial to develop focus if you want to be mentally strong. The successful warrior is the average man with laser-like focus.

Battling The Fear Demons

Everyone has fears and this is inevitable. It is part and parcel of life. However, what separates the winners from the masses who fail is the ability to acknowledge one's fears and push through them.

While conquering one's deepest and darkest fears is not easy, it is definitely worth the effort. As an online marketer, there will be times when the skies seem gloomy and you wonder if it will all work out.

Financial insecurities, temporary setbacks and the usual challenges that life throws at you can be daunting. The majority of beginners will throw in the towel and quit the moment the going gets tough.

They falsely believe that they don't have what it takes to succeed or the journey is just too tough for them. They fear the 'hard yards' and the travails that must be endured for one to see success. They quit out of fear.

But you're different because you know better. When it comes to fear, you really only have 2 choices.

1. **F**orget **E**verything **A**nd **R**un

    Or

2. **F**ace **E**verything **A**nd **R**ise

The choice is quite obvious. While the first one will be easy, it will leave you stranded in the muck and mire of mediocrity. Your dreams and goals will die from strangulation by fear.

Choose the second option and you'll push past your fear with grim determination. When you come out on the other side, you'll be emotionally stronger, mentally tougher and you'll taste the fruits of success.

There is no other way. You only have 2 options. Choose the second one. Everything you want is on the other side of fear.

In this guide we'll look at 5 of the most common fears that plague most online marketers and how you can calm your beating heart.

1. Fear of the Unknown

This is probably one of the biggest fears that entrepreneurs face. When you're starting your own business, while you may have done your homework and prepared the best you can, there will ALWAYS be a certain degree of uncertainty. That's just the way it is.

You must always remember that you can't discover new lands if you're afraid to lose sight of the shore. You have to push through and go with your heart, even if it's beating uncontrollably fast.

Sometime in 1999, there was a movie called "3 Kings". In one scene in the movie, a young soldier who was feeling afraid would approach Sergeant Major Archie Gates (George Clooney) with a question and he'd reply... *"The way this works is... You do the thing you're scared sh*tless of and you get the courage after you do it. Not before you do it."*

This is very true and it applies across the board. If you're worried that you may not have the skills to create an online business, go ahead and do it anyway. Then learn as you go along.

You must have the faith to take the first step even when you can't see the whole staircase. The best way to put an end to your fear of the unknown is to have faith.

You must believe in yourself and what you're trying to achieve. There are thousands of people who come online in droves hoping to make quick and easy money. Most of them fail and quit.

The road to online success is paved with the corpses of the many who have tried and quit. They quit because they didn't believe in themselves and they let fear take over.

Like John Stewart Mill said, "One person with belief is equal to a force of ninety-nine who only have interest."

The next time you have doubts and fears, ask yourself why you're feeling them. Maybe you've been making a stable income online but you're worried about quitting your day job because of the security it provides.

By asking yourself why you have this fear, you'll understand that what you really fear is that you might have no money in case your online business dries up.

Now you'll be able to make plans such as saving up enough money that will last you six months in case of any unexpected setbacks. This is a plan of action.

If you do not analyze your fears and all you do is let them control you and hold you back, your life will become stagnant and in almost all cases, there will be retrogression.

The only way to progress is to keep moving forward whether or not you have fears.

2. The Fear of Failure

This is another major fear that paralyzes so many marketers from taking action on their goals and dreams. The fear of failure has stopped more people in their tracks than any other fear.

Usually this fear is disguised in many different ways. If you worry that all your efforts will go to waste when your online efforts earn you no money, that's a fear of failure. Most people say that they just 'don't want to waste their time on something that won't work.'

The hard truth is that you'll never know unless you try. It may take you 3 years to build an online business that's making you six figures a year. But guess what? If you don't try because you're scared that you'll fail, the time is going to pass anyway.

The 3 years will go by and chances are your life will probably be the same. Whereas if you had moved forward with your goals, you just might be in the six figure income category.

A lot of people fear failure because it will make them look foolish in front of their friends and family. They do not want to endure criticism or sneers from their peers.

This fear is really unnecessary. What others think of you should be the least of your concerns. In fact, you may notice that when you try to better yourself and do things that others don't do, your friends and family will probably be your hardest critics and they'll call it 'concern' or 'tough love.'

The truth of the matter is that you making progress and achieving your goals shines a spotlight on their failures. It makes them feel threatened and the only way for them to feel better is to drag you down to their level so that the status quo can be maintained.

This is life and by understanding that what others think of you is none of your business, this fear of looking foolish will disappear all on its own.

Lao Tzu once said, *"Care about what other people think and you will always be their prisoner."*

The best way to deal with the fear of failure is to ask yourself what could possibly go wrong. Now plan out what countermeasures you can take to prevent your endeavors from failing.

Spend time visualizing yourself pushing past obstacles and succeeding. Repeat this visualization process daily... and even a couple of times a day. This will give you faith and belief in yourself to keep going forward.

3. The Fear That You Are Not Good Enough

This fear arises when one has failed several times throughout life. Many people do not do well academically while in school because they had no natural affinity to the subjects they were learning.

The girl who was gifted at art probably failed at math and science and couldn't go further than high school. This failure may make her feel like she can't succeed at anything in life... even though she has all the potential to be a successful artist.

The very wise Albert Einstein once said, *"Everyone is a genius. But if you judge a fish by its ability to climb a tree, it will live its whole life believing that it is stupid."*

The point of that statement is that one should not judge themselves based on how they performed in school or previous jobs.

There are countless stories of people who failed many times and finally succeeded beyond their wildest dreams once they found their true calling. Never give up on yourself. Fortune favors the bold.

Usually when you're trying to build an online business, there will be a learning curve that you'll have to go through. This is inevitable.

You will make mistakes. You will buy products that are rubbish... And you will waste time and money. This too is normal and can't be avoided. However, if you quit while at this stage because you feel like you're not good enough, you'll NEVER get better.

You only get better as you keep learning and progressing. Many beginners look at the expert marketers and feel intimidated. They believe that the other guys are smarter, richer and better than them.

Do not compare yourself with others. This is a huge mistake and will always leave you feeling discontented. You may be comparing your beginning with someone else's finish. It's not fair to you and you'll be doing yourself a disservice. All you need to do is focus on being the best that you can be.

Here's the truth. Everybody started off as a beginner. You do not become successful overnight. There is a journey that you have to go through and go through it you must.

Fearing that you'll never amount to much will mean that you have given up before you even started. You must have confidence.

Chalk up every little failure that you encounter along the way as a learning experience. You can't extrapolate from incomplete data. The more you learn, the better you'll get.

The more mistakes you make the better. Failure is not the opposite of success. It is a part of success. You are good enough. You've always been. You just need to believe it.

4. The Fear That You're Late or Too Old

This is another big one. You may have heard terms like 'Article marketing is dead... or 'The good ol' days are over'... 'You're too old to start a business'... But are these statements even true?

Of course not. While some methods may come and go, building a business online is here to stay and every single day there are people reaching their income goals. It's never too late to start and now is as good a time as any.

You're also never too old to set new goals or dream new dreams. Stan Lee created his first hit comic close to his 39th birthday. Henry Ford was 45 when he created the Model T car. Ray Croc only started MacDonald's at the age of 52 and Colonel Sanders was 62 when he franchised KFC.

As you can see, people have succeeded in life at all ages. You're never too old. So cast this fear aside and pursue your dreams today.

"The best time to plant a tree was 20 years ago. The second best time is now." – Chinese proverb

5. Limiting Beliefs

Just when you were expecting another fear, you've been hit with 'limiting beliefs'… It may be surprising but it's true. There are many people who have been held back from success because of their own beliefs.

There is an emotional disconnect within them. The reason for this is that while growing up, we formed our beliefs based on what we saw, what we heard and what we were told.

One good example will be overweight people who feel like they're 'destined' to be fat. Their parents, siblings, relatives and everyone close to them is overweight so they buy into the story that they are naturally predisposed to obesity.

While to a certain extent it could be true because some people have a naturally slower metabolism, the truth of the matter is that food choices, eating habits, attitudes towards food, etc. are often passed down from parents to the kids.

Because of this, all they ever knew about food and eating is what they saw and heard. If they decided to eat clean, exercise more and watch their calories, they'd definitely lose all the excess pounds and probably end up being the leanest person in their family.

But getting to this stage requires one to overcome their limited thinking and believe that they are worthy of success.

The same applies to people who grew up in poor families where the parents made it look like money was hard to come by or that rich people were evil and greedy... while poor people were generous and kind.

With beliefs like these, their subconscious mind will not allow them to build wealth because they wouldn't want to be evil and greedy, would they?

Overcoming your limited self-beliefs is a Herculean task but it can be done. You will need to be proactive and actually be alert to the way you think and correct yourself.

Once you realize that your only limit is you, your life will change and you'll conquer this obstacle. You are worthy of success.

By now you'll realize that fear is **f**alse **e**vidence **a**ppearing **r**eal. The best way to conquer fear is through action. Analyzing why you feel the way you feel is helpful... but nothing beats action when it comes to dispelling fear. Do what you fear most and the fear will vanish.

Never let your fear decide your future. Make a good plan, have contingencies in place and work your plan till you succeed. Even during the darkest hours when everything around you may feel like it's all about to collapse and all your fears are telling you that you're about to fail... dig your heels in and keep pushing forward.

It's always darkest before the dawn. Keep going.

Climb The Staircase That You Can't See

There's a saying that goes, "Faith is seeing light with your heart when all your eyes see is darkness." This is very true and when you're trying to build a business, facing problems, hiccups, disappointments and other 'turbulence' is unavoidable.

Most people quit and run the other way once things seem to not be working out. They lose hope and throw in the towel. They do not believe success is within their reach and they assume that it's not possible.

Why?

Because they've lost faith. There is no other explanation for this. A loss of faith in one's self is the number one reason most people quit on themselves. The promise isn't clear to them so they're not willing to pay the price.

However, the people who are single-minded and cannot see anything but themselves reaching their goal will often weather the storms and obstacles to get to where they want to go... and they almost always reach their goals.

Faith is of paramount importance. **It means taking the first step even when you don't see the whole staircase.**

The 4 tips listed below will help you shore up your faith when doubts come knocking on your door.

- **Visualize your success**

Some people call it the law of attraction. Others call it 'The Secret'. Whatever you want to call it... what really matters is that you do it.

Close your eyes and see yourself reaching your goals and attaining your heartfelt desires. Believe that you'll get them and live with an attitude that your success is just around the corner.

This will keep you feeling upbeat and the constant repetition will give you focus and make you remember why you're doing what you do.

- **Prayer is powerful**

While this may not apply to atheists, if you do believe in God, there is immeasurable power in prayer. You will be placing your faith and hopes in a higher power and this will lift some of the burdens weighing on you.

It doesn't matter what religion you follow. It's the action of having hope and faith that your God will help you which is what truly matters.

- **Read autobiographies of successful people**

It's an excellent idea to read autobiographies of successful people. You'll be able to see how much failure they encountered and how they kept going. You'll be able to identify with them and realize that the path to success is not a smooth one.

If they could achieve success, so can you. This will bolster your faith in yourself… and your faith will be bigger than your fears of failure.

- **Motivate yourself regularly**

The famous motivational speaker, Zig Ziglar once said, "People often say that motivation doesn't last. Well, neither does bathing - that's why we recommend it daily."

He's right. It's easy to lose motivation and faith over time. Once the initial excitement of starting on a new goal starts to get dull, most people quit. By constantly motivating yourself, you'll keep going.

Read books or listen to motivational speakers. While some people will scoff and say that it's all 'feel good' stuff… just know that it will you if you give it a chance.

Building a successful business is not easy. If it was, everybody will do it. So, have faith in yourself and know that if you stay the course, success is inevitable. To succeed, you must first believe that you can… and then you will.

A Tiger Doesn't Lose Sleep Over The Opinions Of Sheep.

Call them what you want... naysayers, haters, wet blankets, etc. but the sad truth is that more dreams have been killed by negative people than anything else.

The truly successful people in life never gave two hoots what other people thought of them. They just carried on focusing on their goals and strived till they made their dreams come true.

When you have a dream or a desire in life, it's imperative that you follow your heart. You only have one life to live and you do not want to reach old age where you have no energy and time left to make your dreams come true.

Having regrets when you're old is sad. Your past desires and dreams will return to haunt you and you'll realize that you could have done so much more or been so much more... but you let yourself get discouraged by those who didn't let you be you.

By now, it will be too late and you'll realize that none of what other people said really mattered... and you should have followed your heart. This is a sad scenario but it plays out daily in thousands of people's lives.

You do not want to end up like them. These six tips below will help you to handle naysayers and not let them get you down.

- **Look at your why**

Only you will know why your dreams are so important to you. Maybe you have a love for art and a natural inclination towards it but your parents want you to be a doctor.

Maybe you have a desire to start your own business but your wife is skeptical and thinks that your day job provides more security.

What are you going to do?

If you know why you're doing what you do, you'll push ahead despite what others tell you. The promise will be clear to you and you'll go against your critics.

- **Remember the bamboo tree**

There is a story about the Chinese bamboo. Once you plant the seed, you'll need to water the soil for 5 years. During these 5 years, nothing will happen. However, on the 5th year, a shoot will sprout out from the ground.

Once that happens, over the next 6 weeks, it will grow over 80 feet tall. That's amazing.

The same applies to your goals. It may seem like ages to get there and of course, people will be hinting at you that you might as well quit. Yet, if you persist, once you take off, your success will be massive.

- **Get motivated**

When you're feeling down because people have poured water on your dreams or told you that you're destined to fail, do listen to motivational videos or read motivational books to pick yourself up.

- **Know that it's all turbulence**

When a plane takes off from the ground, many times it will face turbulence as it rises above the weather to reach cruising altitude. In the same vein, the beginning stages of getting to your goal will be tough, but once you get there, it will most often be smooth sailing.

- **Success turns naysayers into supporters**

It's a fact that the same people who laughed at you and mocked you will become your supporters once you make it.

They'll ask you for tips and advice to help themselves achieve success just like you. If you build a successful business, people who doubted you will even ask you for a job. That's just the way the world is.

- **Understand the psychology behind it**

Lastly, you need to understand that when you pursue your dreams, you are like a threat to others. You determination to follow your own path and live life according to your own rules shines a spotlight on the failures of those around you.

It forces people to realize that they quit on themselves or did not do enough. The only way that they can feel better is to pull you down so that you can be a failure just like them.

They may make you feel like they're doing it out of concern. But the truth of the matter is that they're afraid you'll succeed... because if you do, it'll mean that they could have followed their dreams and succeeded too.

Always follow your warrior heart and don't allow the negativity from others to dull your sparkle or your desires.

Weight Loss Is Simpler Than You Think

It is extremely common to gain weight when you devote all your time to work at the expense of everything else. Anyone who has tried to build a business online will realize just how time consuming it is.

It is quite a journey to go from the newbie stage to the level where you earn profits while you sleep… Or live the laptop lifestyle where you make thousands of dollars in twenty minutes while you lie back on some sun-kissed tropical beach.

Most marketers are at the stage where they're struggling to make it work. They let their health slide. They barely exercise. They develop poor eating habits, drink too much coffee and sleep at odd hours.

While it may not seem like a big deal, the pounds will slowly start creeping in. You'll start gaining weight, your metabolism will drop, your energy levels will dip and while your income levels may climb, you will be inviting potential health problems into your life.

This is a very real scenario and many marketers struggle to get their weight under control once they realize how far they've let themselves go. They then put themselves through ridiculous diets or decide to go crazy at the gym.

It all feels torturous and they often quit and resign themselves to being fat. It really doesn't have to be that way. You can be lean and fit while building your online business.

Now you're going to learn 8 simple weight loss tips that will keep you from gaining unnecessary weight. The most important thing to know is that **80 percent of your results come from your diet**.

Just by paying attention to what you eat, you'll be able to prevent the weight gain. After all, you only want to see your income go up and not the numbers on the weighing scale.

In the fitness industry, there is a saying, *"Abs are made in the kitchen, not the gym."*

It just means that your diet is much more important than exercise when it comes to staying lean. You absolutely can't out-exercise a bad diet.

Before going further, we need to talk about something very important... **Your Attitude.**

Most people are impatient and want results fast. Your goal should be different. You should be in this for the long haul. Since you're trying to build a business online, in most cases, you'll be crunched for time.

You just can't afford to spend hours at the gym. Some of the top marketers are so busy that they can only spare time to exercise thrice a week.

So the goal here will be to make gradual improvements over time. As long as you're taking the right steps, you will see results gradually. Instead of struggling with a lemonade diet for 3 weeks, you could follow simpler steps that will get you to the same results in about 5 weeks.

Time is your greatest ally and since your focus is on marketing instead of looking like a Greek God, there is no real rush here. In fact, the slow approach is far more effective in the long run than the short bursts that most people try to do. You're creating healthy habits that will last you a lifetime.

Now let's look at what you need to do.

1. Cut the carbs

This single action alone will make a HUGE difference in your weight. Studies have shown that a diet that restricts carb intake is far more effective than a diet that restricts calorie intake.

First, you'll need to know what your daily calorie numbers should be. You can find that out here: http://www.freedieting.com/tools/calorie_calculator.htm

Now that you know what your calorie deficit should be, your focus should be to get most of your calories from protein and fats. Do not worry about consuming fats. You need to eat fat to lose fat. It may sound contradictory but it's true.

Once your body realizes that it's getting a regular intake of fat, it will be more willing to burn its fat stores since there is no real need to retain fat unnecessarily.

As long as you're at a caloric deficit, you will lose weight. Just ensure that you're consuming 50 grams or less of carbs. This is crucial.

The goal here is to go for 3 to 5 days with a very low carb intake and then follow up with a day where you consume carbs as normal. This is known as a re-feed day or 'cheat' day.

When you consume carbs again after a few days of minimal carbohydrate intake, you'll replenish your body's glycogen stores and give your metabolic rate a boost. Your body will not go into 'starvation mode' where it stubbornly clings on to its fat stores.

In fact, it will start burning more fat now that you have elevated your metabolism again. This method of eating is known as 'carb cycling' and it's used by fitness models all over the world to stay lean and ripped.

As an online marketer, this is not a huge change to make. You'll just be eating a little less daily because of the 500 calorie deficit required… and you'll be consuming less carbs.

It will be slightly difficult initially… but it's not as difficult as switching to a paleo diet or an Atkins diet that takes things to an extreme. All you need to do is switch some of your carb foods to protein foods.

Make gradual changes and you'll find it more bearable. Inch by inch, life is a cinch. Yard by yard, life is hard.

Do note: Of all the 8 tips listed in this book, <u>this is the most important one as far as losing weight goes</u>. If you just get this tip right, you will lose weight. *Your diet is of paramount importance to weight loss.*

2. Intermittent fasting

The second tip to weight loss is intermittent fasting, also known as IF. This is a method of eating that doesn't require you to do much other than eat at different times.

Once you have switched to a carb cycling method of eating, you will need to combine it with intermittent fasting to accelerate your weight loss.

In simple words, intermittent fasting has two windows. There is the eating window and the fasting window. In most cases, the eating window is 8 hours and the fasting window is 16 hours… and in total, that's a day.

All your calories will need to be consumed during the eating window. For example, if you start your day having breakfast at 8 am, your last meal for the day should end at 4pm. That's your 8 hour eating window. <u>You can't eat anything after that</u> but you can drink water.

By doing this, your body will have much more time to tap into its fat stores for fuel since it has not much food left to burn. Intermittent fasting when combined with carb cycling is extremely potent at shedding the excess pounds.

You'll need to decide for yourself when you want to start your eating window. Some people absolutely need breakfast when they wake… while others prefer sleeping with a full stomach.

There are no hard and fast rules here. As long as you eat within the window, it doesn't matter when you start your first meal. An interesting point to note is that the smaller your eating window, the more fat you'll lose.

For example, if your eating window is 5 or 6 hours, it will be more effective than an 8 hour window because your body has more time to tap into its fat stores for fuel.

Another point to note is that you will not be starving yourself. After all, you are getting all the calories you need for the day. You're just getting them in a shorter time frame.

Give intermittent fasting a try and you'll see how effective it is. Initially it will be tough for the first week or so, but once you get the hang of it, your body will adapt and the fat will melt off.

3. Get enough sleep

You absolutely must get enough sleep every day. It is very common for marketers to burn the candle at both ends and sacrifice sleep to get more work done. Once in a while is fine… but this should not become a habit.

A lack of sleep indirectly leads to weight gain. You become more stressed out and your body releases the stress hormone cortisol. You'll end up feeling hungry or binge eating for no real reason.

Get 7 to 8 hours of sleep. Some people may be able to function well with just 5 or 6 hours. It all depends on the individual. Just know that if you're struggling to wake up, you need more sleep.

4. Fasted cardio

This is another simple but very effective tip. When you wake up in the morning, your body is in a fasted state and your glycogen levels are low.

This is the best time to do some light exercise. Just 20 to 30 minutes will do. It could be walking, cycling, swimming or any cardio activity.

The key point to note is that it has to be at an intensity that allows you to break a light sweat but not one where you're gasping for breath.

For example, if you're doing a brisk walk, you should be able to comfortably hold a conversation. That's a good pace to maintain. What really matters is that you do this exercise on an empty stomach.

Your body will tap into its fat stores for fuel because there is no food in the belly for it to use. You'll be burning fat immediately.

So, if you can spare 20 to 30 minutes in the morning, go for a brisk walk and over time, you'll have lost more weight and also feel more energetic.

5. Shorter but higher intensity workouts

As was mentioned earlier, marketers generally do not have much time. Those with day jobs and family commitments have even less time. This is NOT a problem when it comes to exercise.

All too often we hear people say that they *'just don't have time to exercise.'*

While this may be true to a certain extent, there is absolutely no doubt that anyone can spare 10 minutes to exercise. Here's the catch. The workout has to be at maximum intensity.

In fact, you could workout for just 15 minutes thrice a week and be very fit. The goal here is to train at maximum intensity. You want to aim for full body workouts or training methods that are exhausting.

One good example would be sprints. A 10-minute interval workout with you sprinting for 1 minute followed by a rest of 1 minute repeated over and over till the time is up will be far more effective than a 45 minute slow jog.

You'd be surprised to know that even 4 minutes can put you in fat burning mode. Do check out what the Tabata Protocol is and try to do it if you're interested.

A 15-minute workout is 1 percent of your day. Anyone can spare time for it.

6. Eat Foods That Burn Fat

Some foods have been shown to burn more fat than others due to the thermogenic effect of food and even the properties of the food. Below you'll find a list. Do include these foods in your diet.

- Avocado

- Organic Apple Cider Vinegar

- Green Tea

- Broccoli

- Healthy Eggs

- Flax Seeds

- Hot Peppers

- Chicken Breast

- Greek Yogurt

- Salmon

- Onions

- Blueberries

- Cinnamon

- Spinach

- Olive Oil

7. Drink Lots of Water

This is a very simple tip. The body needs water to stay hydrated and metabolize fat. Set a timer on your watch to go off once every hour. Drink a glass of water when the timer goes off. Easy and consistent.

Drink a glass of water before every meal. It will make you feel fuller and you will be less inclined to eat more than you need to. This one action can really help to curb your appetite.

8. Have a Food Journal

Write down everything you eat and drink for the day. Now you have a written record that will show you where you're slipping up. All you need to do is replace unhealthy food choices with healthier ones.

The goal here is to make small positive changes that are easy to comply with. Go from 3 sodas a day to 2 a day. Don't suddenly cut out all 3 and switch to unsweetened green tea. Compliance will be a nightmare and you'll probably end up drinking 5 sodas a day. Go slow and make gradual progress.

If you follow these 8 tips, your weight loss progress will skyrocket. Since you lack time, what you do must count. These are some of the most effective weight loss tips out there.

They do not require massive changes or too much time. Any online marketer can follow these tips without disrupting their life.

So, implement these tips and you'll look better, feel better and be proud of your body.

From Ideal Weight To A Six Pack

In this chapter, you'll be given the exact information to get a six pack. It's easier than most people realize.

Ideally, you should have used the tips from the previous chapter to reach your ideal weight. You can find out your ideal weight here - http://www.calculator.net/ideal-weight-calculator.html

You really have no business struggling with sit-ups and talking about a six pack if you're 30 pounds overweight. Getting a six pack requires you to first be at your ideal weight.

From there, you'll lower your bodyfat percentage till you reach the single digits. In bodybuilding, they call it being vascular. Men will see their six pack once they're at 6 to 9 percent bodyfat. Women will see it when they're at 16 to 19 percent bodyfat.

So how do you get there?

Calories

As an online marketer, you probably are too busy to slave away at the gym for hours. The truth is that you really do not need to. All you need to do is follow the tips that you learned earlier to keep your body in fat burning mode.

You must monitor your calories very closely. You can see the calculation below.

> To see a 2-pack – (Bodyweight in pounds X 13) calories
>
> To see a 4-pack – Bodyweight in pounds X 12) calories
>
> To see a 6-pack – (Bodyweight in pounds X 11) calories

Basically, you're taking your weight in pounds and multiplying it by the numbers shown. So, if you weigh 160 pounds, you should be consuming not more than 2,080 calories a day till you see your 2-pack, which is your top 2 abs muscles. Then drop your calorie intake to your current weight multiplied by 11.

<u>Make sure you go progressively</u>. Do not start off with your bodyweight and multiply it by 10 just so you can get your six pack faster. You'll just end up hitting a plateau and see no progress.

Training

Now that the calorie part is taken care of, you'll need to make sure that most of your workouts are at maximum intensity.

You must be gasping and struggling as you workout. Nothing but your very best! This will create a situation known as EPOC – excess post-exercise oxygen consumption.

Once you reach this stage, your body will be in fat burning mode for 10 to 14 hours after your workout. The fat will just melt off. Do full-body workouts that include exercises such as:

- Deadlifts

- Pull-ups

- Lunges

- Squats

- Snatches

- Mountain climbers

- Burpees

- Bench presses

- Hanging leg raises

These are compound movements. It's a great idea to use weights. Unlike earlier when you were just trying to shed the excess pounds, now you're trying to burn the last and most stubborn layer of fat.

You only need to do about 20 to 30 minutes. There's no need for 45-minute or 60-minute workouts. Short fast workouts are what matters.

Always lift as much weight as you can fast and with good form. If your form is wobbly or you're slow, the weights are too heavy. Use lighter weights that are manageable but still challenging.

Diet

By now, you should have instilled some discipline in your eating. Here's an important point to note. When trying to shed excess fat, as long as you're at a caloric deficit, you'll lose weight.

What you eat while important, is not didn't really have much of an impact. You could sneak in junk food now and then and still lose weight as long as you consumed less calories than you expend.

To get six pack abs, **your diet will be a lot less forgiving**. Not all calories are made equal. You'll need to clean up your diet as much as you can.

A bar of chocolate that has 200 calories is a lot more detrimental than a slice of steak that is also 200 calories. While the numbers are the same, the chocolate will cause your blood sugar levels to spike.

Your body will release insulin which will lead to weight gain… or at the very least, it will be much more difficult to burn off the last stubborn layer of fat on your lower abdomen that really doesn't want to leave.

Avoid processed foods and dairy as much as you can. Stick to single ingredient foods such as broccoli, chicken breast, etc. Your body can only take in so many calories and every calorie has to count.

You should consume most of your calories in protein and fat. This is known as a ketogenic diet. You must eat fat to lose fat. Add extra virgin olive oil or cold pressed coconut oil during your food preparation.

As long as there is sufficient fat and proteins in your diet and about 50 grams of carbs daily, you'll reach your six pack within 4 to 7 weeks. To really speed things up, incorporate intermittent fasting into your program and have a 5 or 6 hour eating window.

Another thing to be aware of is that for each gram of carbohydrates that you consume, your body will hold on to 3 grams of water. So, if on one particular day you consume more carbs, you weight will rise the next day due to water retention.

You can solve this problem by drinking a lot more water on that day to flush out the excess water. The same applies if you eat foods high in salt. It seems contradictory that one should drink more water to reduce water retention. But that's how it is.

That's really all there is to it. You do not need to spend countless hours at the gym or do thousands of sit-ups. **3 to 4 short but intense workouts a week is more than enough to get your six pack**.

Building Muscle and Gaining Mass

Generally, it's best to get a six pack first before you attempt to bulk up. While getting a six pack requires you to be at a caloric deficit, building muscle and gaining mass requires you to be at a caloric surplus.

As an online marketer, you probably don't have the time to dedicate to working out one body part a day. So, you need a split.

Once again, the goal is 3 workouts a week – about 30 to 40 minutes each. You really do not need to go above that. You can if you want to, but it isn't necessary. Let's look at an example of a 3-day split.

Monday – Legs/calves

Tuesday – Rest

Wednesday – Chest/shoulders/triceps

Thursday – Rest

Friday – Back/biceps/forearms

That's an excellent split and it's manageable. There are so many different exercises to target each muscle. It would be best to do research and vary your workouts.

Generally, these are the most crucial and effective exercises. If all you did were these exercises, you would be fine.

- Legs – Barbell squats, calf raises, dumbbell lunges
- Biceps – Hammer curls, EZ bar curls, incline hammer curls, bicep curls
- Triceps – Skullcrushers, push-ups, triceps pushdowns, close grip bench press
- Chest – Barbell bench press, incline bench press, dips, incline dumbbell flyes
- Forearms – Seated wrist curls, wrist rollers, farmer's walk

- Back – Deadlifts, wide grip pull-ups, single arm dumbbell rows, snatches

- Shoulders – Front/side/rear lateral raises, Arnold press

How many reps and sets?

All you need to do is 8 to 12 reps per exercise for 4 to 5 sets. Lift as much weight as you can to barely make these reps. You want to be challenging yourself.

You do not always need to train to failure. Training to failure is a strategy that should be employed once every 3 workouts.

Training to failure means that on your last set of each exercise, you keep doing reps until a point where you just can't do another one more rep. Your muscles will be burning and all good form goes out the window.

This will cause micro-tears in your muscles and when the scars heal, there'll be more muscle tissue. **Do note that you should take a 1 week break every 8 weeks.** Do not exercise during this entire week. Let your body heal.

As far as nutrition goes, **you should multiply your bodyweight in pounds by 20 to know how many calories you should be consuming.** It's a good idea to get most of your calories from clean food that is nutritious.

But sometimes, that can be difficult and tiring. It's perfectly fine to eat some junk food to meet the calorie count. This is known as a 'dirty bulk.'

Will you gain weight? Yes... but you'll also gain muscle. Do not worry too much about gaining fat. You can do a 'cut' later where you burn off the excess fat. You already know what you need to know to lose weight.

Ideally, you should bulk for 2 or 3 months and then do a cut where you go on a caloric deficit and burn fat. Keep your diet clean during this period and do not do more than 2 or 3 high intensity workouts a week… and keep them within the 15 to 20 minute duration.

You just want to boost your metabolism so that your body goes into fat burning mode. As long as your diet is on point and clean, you'll shed the excess pounds but now you'll have more muscle mass.

Do not let yourself get too overweight before you decide to do a cut. Monitor your weight closely.

Some men find it extremely hard to bulk up. These are usually ectomorph body types with a high metabolic rate. If you face this issue, you'll need to aim for a 1,000 to 2,000 calorie a day surplus over and above the number you calculated earlier.

You'll feel sick of eating but it's a necessary evil. All cardio training should be limited to just walking for about 20 minutes twice or thrice a week.

Never workout more than thrice a week. You can even workout twice a week and it may yield better results. Less is more… and while it seems counterintuitive, this is what an ectomorph needs to do.

As with all things, consistency is the most important thing. Since it's just 3 times a week and the workouts are about 30 minutes long, it's definitely manageable.

How much muscle can I hope to gain?

According to Lyle Macdonald's Natural Lean Muscle Mass Gain Model… this is what you can expect. It's a pretty accurate guide.

Year 1 - 20-25 pounds (2 pounds per month)

Year 2 - 10-12 pounds (1 pound per month)

Year 3 - 5-6 pounds (.5 pound per month)

Year 4 and on - 2-3 pounds (not worth calculating)

As you can see, it takes time to build muscle and as the years pass, it gets more difficult. So, tailor your expectations accordingly and stay the course. Consistency is the key. If you can't be consistent, you can't be anything.

Before you start with weights…

Here's something that most gym trainers will not tell you. Before you even sign up for a gym membership or start training with weights, make sure you put yourself through about 8 weeks of solid bodyweight training.

There are so many beginners who do bicep curls and hammer curls at the gym… but they can't do a single pull-up. Ask them to do 30 push-ups at a go and they struggle.

Build a strong foundation by doing as much bodyweight training as you can. Your muscles and ligaments will get used to resistance training... and you'll be amazed to discover that even guys who are built like a house, struggle with bodyweight exercises such as the V-sit, muscle up, human flag, archer push-ups, etc.

Go on YouTube and find as many different bodyweight exercises that you can and do them till you are good at them and much stronger. Now you have a solid foundation in resistance training... you're ready for weights at the gym.

Don't neglect your posture and flexibility

Make sure you stretch often and always maintain good posture. As a marketer who spends hours in front of the computer, do make sure you stretch your neck, shoulders, back and do head rotations.

This will prevent chronic issues from arising. Get up off your seat for 5 minutes every hours and do some stretches. This is very important. If you can, practice yoga and Pilates. This will be very beneficial in the long run.

Resistance training will make your muscles tighter. There will be a loss of range of motion. To solve this problem, do some light stretching daily.

A Warrior Watches His Money

As far as getting lean, fit and muscular go, you already know all you need to know. Now you need to know an important truth – How to manage your money and when is the right time to quit your day job.

The majority of people who try and make money online do so because they wish to quit their day job. They hate the commute, the lack of freedom, their unreasonable bosses, their backstabbing colleagues... and the list of woes goes on.

It all seems so nice to be able to work from home. No commute. Freedom to do what you want, when you want and nobody to boss you around. It's fantastic.

The big question is... **When do you quit your day job?**

Many marketers make a huge mistake here and quit their day job way too early. They decide to give internet marketing their full attention and it's either make it or break it. They actually believe that they're bold and taking the right action.

Nothing could be further from the truth.

Make it or break it? Almost all the time, these marketers break it and fail on an epic level. They become broke, in debt and finally end up getting another job. They then feel bitter and give up on internet marketing.

What they don't realize is that they could have made it if they only knew when to quit their day job... and this is what they should have looked out for.

- **What's your number?**

Your number refers to the amount of money you need to survive every month. A good estimate will be your current salary multiplied by 1.5.

If you are earning this amount consistently every month for 5 to 6 months, you are ready to quit. The reason it is 1.5 and not one is because your income can fluctuate wildly at times and the extra 0.5 is just to take up the slack should you earn less any single month.

You do not want to be in a situation where you can't afford your rent just because your website was down for a week due to some issue.

- **Money is oxygen to your business**

You need money to build an online business. Your day job will provide you that money to invest in your business. As long as your online business is incapable of sustaining itself from its own earnings, you are not ready to quit your day job yet.

Use a portion of your monthly salary to invest in your business. Work at your day job while you build your fortune. Once you are raking in the dollars, you can toss in your resignation.

- **Can you do both effectively?**

This is an interesting question. Many people do not really hate their day job. They just hate their salary. If you have an online income that's making you an extra two thousand a month, life at your job may suddenly seem much better since you have more cash now.

If that's the case and you like your day job and colleagues, there's really no need to quit. You can automate and outsource your business so that you can have both a job and an online income.

- **Your six month nest egg**

Before quitting your day job, make sure you have at least 6 months of your current salary saved up. This will be a buffer in the event that there is an emergency or if your business suddenly fails.

You'll have time to fix the problems or at the very least, find a new job.

- **Insurance and medical benefits**

Most jobs have some form of insurance or medical benefits such as dental coverage, etc. Make sure you're earning enough online to cover all these costs. There's more than just a monthly wage that you should be looking at.

- **Is your spouse working?**

Yes, even warriors get married and if you are, does your spouse have a job? If they do, there is at least a backup source of income should things not go as planned.

Do remember all these points before you quit your day job to do internet marketing full-time. If you do it right, you'll ease smoothly and successfully into being your own boss and not working for the man anymore. It's really a life-changing event.

The Biggest Secret To Making Money Online

This one is so obvious yet most beginners don't seem to get it. Here's the secret… **You only make money when you sell.**

That's it. No matter what type of marketing you're doing, you ONLY make money when you sell something. You could be doing affiliate marketing or ecommerce or product creation… Whatever it may be, you still only make money when you sell.

Even for those providing services such as graphic design, content creation, etc. You make money by selling your services.

You must focus on selling! Like they say, "Always be selling."

There's just no getting away from this fact. No amount of learning or buying products and software will ever make you money online if you do not sell. Read that again.

It is so important. You must avoid getting infected with shiny object syndrome.

What's shiny object syndrome?

'Shiny object syndrome' is a term commonly used in the internet marketing scene to refer to marketers who keep buying new products that hit the market but never take any action on the info that they buy.

All they seem to do is buy and buy and buy… but they never apply what they learn. They may give some of the methods a try but before anything can gain traction, they quit and start something new.

In the make money online space, thousands of products keep coming out. They have flashy sales pages, sales copy that's hyped up and promises easy profits that will give you the lifestyle of a celebrity rapper.

In reality, most of the products are rehashed and untested theory that just don't work. However, thousands of beginners have spend a ton of their money on these products and never make a cent in return.

Shiny object syndrome is one of the biggest reasons why most people online fail to make money online. They are so busy buying that they never do any selling. The 5 tips below will help you to vaccinate yourself against this 'syndrome' that kills your chances at online success.

- **Most of it is noise**

That's right. Most of the products are released by serial product creators who do not practice what they preach. You need to watch what these marketers are doing instead of what they're saying. The money is in product creation and selling these products.

Forget about the hype and loopholes that their systems promise. If their methods were so good, they'd be doing it themselves but most of them never practice what they preach.

- Focus on just one method

Pick a method that is sustainable in the long run. For example, affiliate marketing, ecommerce, etc. Pick just one method and stick to it till you make it work. Only get products related to what you're doing and nothing more.

The method you choose must be a proven business model and not some sneaky loophole that may never work.

- **Stick to proven products and reputable sellers**

Do your research and only buy infoproducts or software that has been proven to work or are created by credible sellers. Ask around for reviews and see if anyone has actually benefitted from using these products.

The hard truth is that the majority of products have a very short shelf life because they're neither useful nor effective.

- **Get the right tools only**

It's inevitable to reach a point where you need tools to run your online business. You may need membership software, autoresponders, ecover creators, etc. Always choose one that is good.

Even if the good ones are a little pricey, you should invest in them. Cheaper alternatives may be unreliable and break down. In some cases, the products may not even deliver what they promise.

So exercise due diligence and stick to proven products that have stood the test of time.

- **Segment your emails**

As a marketer you'll be inundated with emails from other marketers. All these emails will usually be for offers screaming for your attention. Unsubscribe from lists that offer no value… and for those lists that you are on, do segment the emails to go into separate folders.

You can check them once in a while when you're free. You'll be less tempted to splurge on new products that you don't need.

Other than these 5 tips, do your best not to buy products that you won't use immediately or within a short while. Do not buy products that you might use 'one day' in the future. In most cases, that one day won't come.

When The Warrior Fails...

You may have read all the self-help books and the autobiographies of men like Abraham Lincoln who failed all their lives and finally succeeded. It all seems so positive and feel good... until you fail.

One of Mike Tyson's most famous quotes is, *"Everybody has a plan until they get punched in the mouth."*

There's just no denying that failure is a bitter pill to swallow. It doesn't matter how many times you fail, you'll still feel that twinge of disappointment or some anger when your best laid plans collapse.

Usually, the most successful people are also the ones who are best at coping with failure. The reason for this is that they fail more than most people but they just never give up. That also means that they do more than most other people who quit the moment failure knocks on their door.

There are many ways to cope with failure but you must understand that it is going to hurt when you fail. Sometimes it may feel like the only thing you ever learn from a failure is that you failed.

While this is not true, it will seem that way. We are all human and no one likes to see their efforts go to waste. It could be a business venture that collapses. Or maybe your relationship with your spouse crumbles and is beyond repair. Maybe your health takes a turn for the worse despite living a healthy lifestyle.

All these are events. Understanding this point makes all the difference between handling failure successfully or letting it break you. Failure is an event, not a person.

Like they say, never let success get to your head and never let failure get to your heart. It will hurt and there will be disappointment… but you must embrace the experience and push forward.

Success is not final and failure is not fatal. As long as you're breathing you still can turn your failures into successes. It's time to discover the 7 secrets that successful people use to cope with failure.

Different individuals may do it differently but the general rule of thumb is this – Failure is always temporary. Failure is not the opposite of success. It is part of success. Now let's look at how you can cope with it when it comes your way... and you can rest assured that it will. So be prepared.

1. Don't take it personally.

This is the biggest mistake that most people make. They blame themselves when things go wrong. Or they blame other people. When you do not separate failure from how you identify yourself, then your self-esteem will drop and you'll be much more tempted to quit.

People usually quit on their dreams because they don't believe that they're capable of achieving what their hearts desire. They feel that it's too hard... and the reason they feel that way is because they may have failed.

For example, when someone is trying to lose weight and watching their diet closely, there will be times when they give in to temptation and eat something they shouldn't. When this happens, they feel guilt and regret that they failed at maintaining their diet.

What do they do then? They toss their diet aside and gorge themselves on food that they're not supposed to. They believe that they lack the self-discipline to stay focused and lose weight... Just because of one temporary lapse in judgment.

This is ridiculous and it's like accidentally dropping your mobile phone once only to pick it up and keep smashing it on the ground over and over because of one accident. It doesn't make sense... and yet people act in a similar way.

When you fail at something, whether it's with your blog or your email marketing or if your latest product launch is a flop, do not assume that you're useless and just throw in the towel. What defines you is how well you rise after falling.

So… the most important point to note is that you should not let failure define you as a person. Always know that you can do better.

2. Learn From Your Mistakes

All the most successful people have learned from their mistakes and try not to repeat them. Failure can also be treated as feedback. If some aspect of your online business fails, ask yourself why this happened.

For example, if your product launch was a flop, there must be a reason why. Was your niche unprofitable? Did the sales page convert poorly? Did you not actively recruit affiliates?

Analysis is very important so that you do not repeat the same errors. This is the only way to make progress and succeed.

Michael Eisner, the Chairman and CEO of the Disney Corporation said, *"Failure is good as long as it doesn't become a habit."* The only way to prevent failure from becoming a habit is to take stock of your situation, learn from your mistakes and adapt.

Try to maintain a certain degree of detachment so that you can evaluate your failure without feeling bitter. Sometimes it might be a good idea to take a break for a short while and come back to it when you're feeling better. Either way, ALWAYS analyze your failures.

3. Stop Dwelling On Your Failures

You may have noticed that all some people can talk about is how life has treated them so badly. No matter what they do, they fail at it due to bad luck or unforeseen circumstances.

We've all seen people like these… and while you may not know why these things happen to them, you know that things like these always seem to happen to people like them.

Harsh but very true. Do not dwell on your failures. Analyze them and move on. You have better things in store for you. Missed out on an opportunity? No worries. Better ones are coming your way.

Product launch flopped? That's ok... the next one will sell thousands. Picked the wrong niche to monetize? No big deal. You now know how to find niches with people waiting to buy stuff. Problem solved.

It is inevitable to lose time, effort and money when something fails. If you keep focusing on what is lost, you'll never be able to focus on what you can gain... and there is so much more out there for you.

Focus on the positive and bury your failures.

4. Model Other Marketers

There's a saying that you should always learn from the mistakes of others because you'll never live long enough to make them all yourself.

When trying to build an online business, instead of believing all the hype that you see in all the infoproducts that flood the market, you'd be better off watching what the successful marketers are doing. Do what they do and not what they say.

Most beginners to online marketing encounter failure repeatedly because they follow untested theory and blindly believe what they read or hear. You have to be smarter than that.

If whatever you're doing seems to be failing, then you need to look at what other marketers who are succeeding are doing… then model them. That alone will reduce your learning curve and put you on the path to online success.

Stop being like a housefly that repeatedly bangs its head on the window hoping to get out when the door is wide open for it to go through.

5. Assess Your Finances

One of the biggest concerns marketers have when they fail is that they've lost money. Creating a product costs money. Testing out ads costs money. Outsourcing costs money. There is no getting away from this.

In fact, to run any business you need money. It's like oxygen for your business and without it, your business will shrivel up and die. So, it's crucial that you have a source of income coming in to tide you over if any online endeavour fails.

Some marketers quit their day jobs to make their online business work. When the business fails and the bills start piling up, they start getting desperate.

At times like these, you just may need to get another job to get back on your feet. Do not feel like you have failed and are doomed to a life of 'working for the man.'

This is just a temporary setback... and like Joel Osteen, always says, "A setback is a set up for a comeback." Go ahead and take that job. It will feel like retrogression but you must understand that even a tiger crouches before it leaps.

Once you have money coming in, the pressure that your finances are causing you will ease. You'll be able to save up some money to keep funding your online business.

That's really how it is. Sometimes you just don't have a choice. Do not throw your efforts down the drain and quit online marketing totally just because you failed a couple of times. As long as you keep learning and doing, success is inevitable.

6. Release the Need for Approval from Others.

This is a very common fear and makes failure seem worse than it really is. People often worry what others will think or say about them when they fail. It's definitely true that you'll have friends and family members who will tell you, *"I told you so!"* when you fail.

Some of them may even take pleasure in it. This is human nature. It could even be your spouse or parents who don't support your dreams. When you fail and see their disapproving looks or hear their sarcastic words, it can seem worse.

The truth of the matter is that you only have one life to live and you need to live it for yourself. It doesn't matter what others say or think about you. Just because others think you're dumb for failing doesn't mean that you're really foolish.

How people see you should have zero impact on how you see yourself. Have faith in yourself and don't pay heed to the naysayers.

7. Take a Break

Time heals all wounds. Sometimes when failure really gets to you, it may be time to take a break and put some space between you and your business. This will help to clear your mind so that you can think objectively.

While taking a break, you can self-reflect and think about your future plans. You may decide to have backup plans to correct any future failures or problems that may crop up.

Take the time to exercise. Research has shown that hard training like boxing, Crossfit, sprinting, etc. help people to release pent up frustration and anger.

This can be therapeutic when coping with failure. Instead of hitting the bottle, you can hit a punching bag or lift heavy weights explosively during CrossFit sessions. Do what suits you best.

What is most important is that you not let failure make you quit. That is the most common consequence of failure. People fail a few times and they quit.

If you read the story of Colonel Sanders, you'd realise that he was turned down 1,009 times before he finally found someone who would use his recipe. Walt Disney was turned down over 300 times before he received financing for Disney World.

By any standards, you could say that these guys were massive failures... **Until they succeeded**. The difference is that they kept going while the masses would have quit long ago. *Would you keep going if you failed a 1,009 times?*

How about 10 times? Most people don't even get past 2 failures. So what if you fail? It's no big deal. You get up, dust yourself and move on. That's the only way to succeed... To keep on keeping on. You can do it.

"I've missed more than 9000 shots in my career. I've lost almost 300 games. 26 times, I've been trusted to take the game winning shot and missed. I've failed over and over and over again in my life. And that is why I succeed." - **Michael Jordan**

What It All Comes Down To

This is a quote by Leonardo da Vinci – "Simplicity is the ultimate sophistication."

It's a fantastic quote that should apply all aspects of your life, especially so when building an online business. Most people make internet marketing more difficult than it really is.

The buy so many products and so much software that they get overwhelmed. Their computer desktop is cluttered with icons and their business is a mess because it's all so chaotic.

Many beginners are also held back from progressing because of their tendency to overcomplicate things. They make the process harder than it is and then feel like it's all too hard for them.

Keep your business simple and it will be successful. It's really not difficult to do this.

- **Be organized**

This is the first step to simplicity. Plan your day beforehand so that you know exactly what tasks to do for that day. Make sure the folders in your computer are well-organized and easy to find.

Keep the most important and often used files on your desktop and clear the rest away into some other folder that's not on your screen.

Get an external storage drive to save all files that you just need to keep as a record. This will save space on your computer and speed things up.

- **Master the fundamentals**

You must master the basics before moving on to more complex tasks. If you do not know the basics of video creation, don't buy the most expensive and complex video editing software that you can find and struggle to figure it out.

Spend time learning the basics till you understand the terminology and the different aspects of video creation. Once you have a firm grasp of the fundamentals, you can take on the more complex tasks.

- **Stick to the basics**

Some people work best with a pen and paper. Some use planners. Others use software like Trello online to stay organized. You just need to use what you're most comfortable with.

If you find it easier to just scribble notes on paper, then do that. Even if it's basic and not all 'techy'... if it works for you, stick to it. There's really no need to master Trello or Evernote just because everyone else is using these. Do what suits you best.

- **Always have a backup plan**

You should do your best to have a Plan B whenever possible. For example, if you're quitting your day job to do online marketing full time, make sure you have at least enough savings to tide you for six months in case of any unforeseen circumstances.

If you blindly quit your day job and your online business does not take off, the financial stress is really going to affect you and take a toll on you mentally and emotionally. You'll be working from a place of desperation.

Keep things simple and plan well in advance.

- **Stay grounded**

When you do succeed online, you'll be tempted to get a bigger house or a better car or more expensive things now that you can afford it. While the occasional reward is good for the soul, do not overdo it.

If you buy a flashy car with high monthly payments that require you to work crazy hours online just to keep up, then you don't own the car. The car owns you.

The same can be said for any material possession that causes you stress because you need to constantly work really hard to afford it.

Live within your means. Do not fall into the trap of buying things you don't need with money that you don't have, to impress people who don't care. It's unnecessary stress.

Keep things as simple as possible in all aspects of your life.

"The cost of a thing is the amount of what I will call life which is required to be exchanged for it, immediately or in the long run." - Henry David Thoreau

Be A Warrior, Not a Worrier

You've reached the end of this book. If you're still reading this, you've done better than most who would have quit halfway.

Now, all you need to do is apply what you've read. While the info in this guide may seem simple, that doesn't make it easy. You'll need to dig deep to keep going when things get hard.

Do reread this book whenever the need arises. Cast your worries aside and have faith in yourself. Aim for balance in your life. Know with resolute confidence that you'll reach your goals.

Once you have faith in yourself, then it's just a matter of putting one foot in front of another and carrying on. There will be no need to rush or feel fear. You're going to reach your destination no matter what.

As long as you take action and do what you need to, you'll truly become a warrior marketer. You'll have your health, your fitness, a super cool body, a successful online business and the knowledge that you did it all without letting anything slide.

This is priceless. Weapons and situations may change... but warriors don't. Stay true to what you learned from this book and you'll be unbeatable.

www.ingramcontent.com/pod-product-compliance
Lightning Source LLC
Chambersburg PA
CBHW070651220526
45466CB00001B/392